# BUILDING THE PYRAMIDS

Carmel Reilly

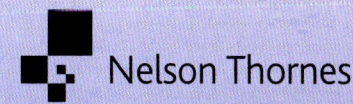

Nelson Thornes

# Nelson Thornes

First published in 2007 by Cengage Learning Australia
www.cengage.com.au

This edition published in 2008 under the imprint of Nelson Thornes Ltd,
Delta Place, 27 Bath Road, Cheltenham, United Kingdom, GL53 7TH

10 9 8 7 6 5 4 3 2
11 10 09 08

Text © 2007 Cengage Learning Australia Pty Ltd ABN 14058280149
(incorporated in Victoria)
Illustrations © 2007 Cengage Learning Australia Pty Ltd ABN 14058280149
(incorporated in Victoria)

The right of Carmel Reilly to be identified as author of this work has been asserted by him/her in accordance with the Copyright, Designs and Patents Act 1988

All rights reserved. No part of this publication may be reproduced or transmitted in any form or by any means, electronic or mechanical, including photocopy, recording or any information storage and retrieval system, without permission in writing from the publisher or under licence from the Copyright Licensing Agency Limited, of 90 Tottenham Court Road, London W1T 4LP.

Any person who commits any unauthorised act in relation to this publication may be liable to criminal prosecution and civil claims for damages.

*Building the Pyramids*
ISBN 978-1-4085-0194-8

Text by Carmel Reilly
Illustrations by Julian Bruere
Edited by Cameron Macintosh
Designed by James Lowe
Series Design by James Lowe
Production Controller Seona Galbally
Photo Research by Fiona Smith
Audio recordings by Juliet Hill, Picture Start
Spoken by Matthew King and Abbe Holmes
Printed in China by 1010 Printing International Ltd

Website www.nelsonthornes.com

Acknowledgements
The author and publisher would like to acknowledge permission to reproduce material from the following sources:
Photographs by Alamy/bygonetimes, p. 3 /Danita Delimont, p. 21 bottom /Frantisek Staud, p. 6 /Visual Arts Library (London), p. 22; iStockphoto.com, p. 7 top /Pierrette Guertin, front cover, p. 5 /Tauno Novek, p. 21 top; Photolibrary.com/Superstock, Inc, p. 7 bottom; The Art Archive/Egyptian Museum Cairo/Dagli Orti, p. 4.

# BUILDING THE PYRAMIDS

CARMEL REILLY

## Contents

| Chapter 1 | **Tombs of the Pharaohs** | 4 |
| Chapter 2 | **Building the Pyramids** | 8 |
| Chapter 3 | **Going Up** | 16 |
| Chapter 4 | **Chambers and Passages** | 18 |
| Chapter 5 | **Finishing Off** | 20 |
| Glossary and Index | | 24 |

# Chapter 1

# TOMBS OF THE PHARAOHS

The great **pyramids** of Egypt were built
more than 4000 years ago
as tombs for the pharaohs, or kings, of the time.

In ancient Egypt, people believed that
when pharaohs died they became gods in the next life.
To be able to do this, the pharaohs needed their bodies.
So their bodies were preserved
and placed somewhere safe when they died.
These preserved bodies were called mummies.

the mummy of Pharaoh Ramesses II

the pyramids of Giza, near Cairo, Egypt

The Egyptians thought that pyramids
would be a safe place to put the mummies of pharaohs.
They believed that placing the mummies
in pyramids would help them to reach heaven,
where they would make their new home.

As well as being tombs for pharaohs,
the pyramids were also wonders of construction.

For thousands of years,
the pyramids were the largest buildings in the world.
It wasn't until the 20th century
that bigger buildings were made.
Even today, there aren't many buildings
that are taller than the pyramids.

Khufu's pyramid

The largest of the pyramids was built for Pharaoh Khufu. It is 138 metres tall, which is more than twice as tall as the Sydney Opera House.

# Chapter 2

# BUILDING THE PYRAMIDS

Because the pyramids were so big, it took a lot of time and work to build them. Many **engineers**, **architects**, **masons** and artists were employed over many years to build each one.

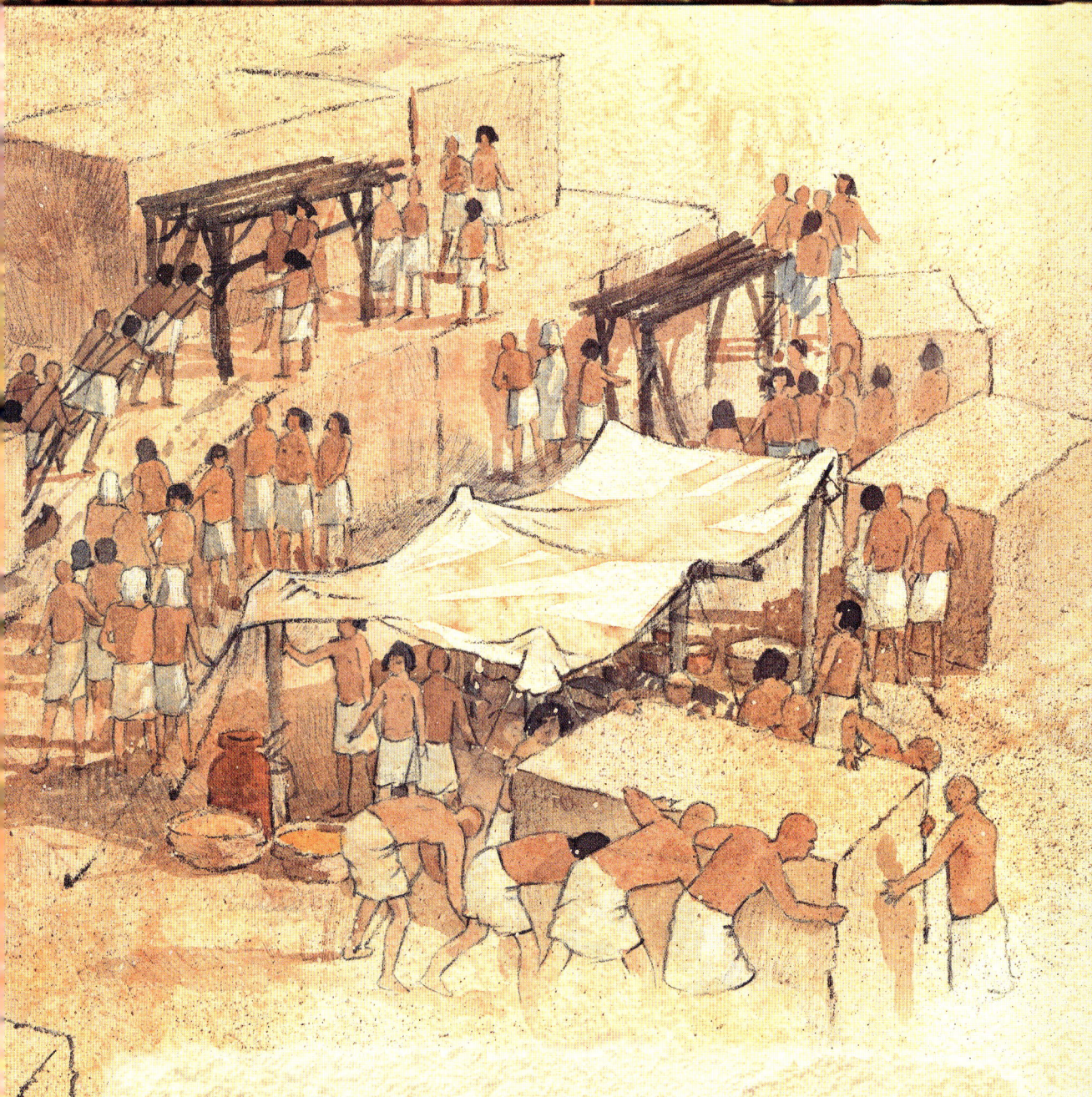

Thousands of **labourers** also worked on the pyramids each year.
The labourers were mostly local farmers who gave up a few months of their time each year to help out.

# The First Step

The first step in building a pyramid was to pick a site.
Then architects and engineers worked together
to design the pyramid
and make sure that it would be strong and safe.

Not all pyramids were the same.
Some were taller than others.

Some had different angles because their bases were larger than others.

All of them were constructed differently inside, too. Many were made up of stone only, while some were filled with a mix of stone, mud bricks, and even sand.

# Cutting the Stone

Building work began when the pyramid was designed.

There was a lot of stone in Egypt, and builders of pyramids often found supplies of stone nearby that they could use.

The Egyptians had no machinery or iron tools.
Stone masons had to dig the stone from the ground
and then cut it into large blocks
using only copper and stone hand tools.

# Bringing the Stone to the Site

After the stones for the pyramid were cut, workers moved them to the pyramid site. This was not an easy job because most stones weighed more than two tonnes — as much as a small truck.

The Egyptians didn't have the use of the wheel, so each stone had to be dragged to the site on a sled pulled by gangs of labourers.

Along the way, someone would sprinkle water on the ground to help the sled move more easily.

Sometimes, the stones were brought to the site on boats along the nearby Nile River.

# Chapter 3

# GOING UP

The stones for the base of the pyramid were placed straight onto the ground.

However, because it was too hard for the labourers to lift the heavy stones higher, ramps were built so that the stones could be dragged up to the next level.

When each level was finished,
the size of the ramp was increased
so that work could begin on the next level.
Sometimes, ramps were built
between the levels as well.

This process went on until the levels
reached a peak at the top
and the pyramid was finished.

# Chapter 4

# CHAMBERS AND PASSAGES

As the pyramid was being built, **chambers** and passages were constructed inside.

One of the chambers was made for the mummy of the pharaoh.

The other chambers were for all the goods that the pharaoh would need in the next life.

The passages allowed the workers to get in and out of the pyramid to work on the chambers.

# Chapter 5

# FINISHING OFF

When the core of the pyramid was finished, the outside was covered in a white stone called **limestone.** The peak of the pyramid was capped in gold.

At the same time, labourers, masons and artists finished off the work inside.

Each chamber was lined with fine stone.

The walls were painted with scenes from the pharaoh's life, or the building of the pyramid.

When the inside and the outside
of the pyramid were finished,
beautiful art works and goods for the pharaoh's next life
were put in the chambers.
Then, the mummy was placed in its special chamber.

Finally, the passages to the chambers were filled with huge stones, and the openings were closed off and covered in limestone.

## Glossary

**architects**  people who design buildings

**chambers**  rooms designed for a special purpose

**engineers**  people who use scientific knowledge to solve practical problems

**labourers**  people who do heavy, unskilled work

**limestone**  a white stone used for building, and used to make cement

**masons**  people who build with stone

**pyramids**  structures with square bases and sloping sides that meet centrally at the top

## Index

architects  8, 10
artists  8, 21

Egypt  4, 12
engineers  8, 10

labourers  9, 15, 16, 21
limestone  20, 23

masons  8, 21
mummies  4, 5, 18, 22

Pharaoh Khufu  7
pharaohs  4, 5, 6, 18, 21